This book

belongs to

Grosspietsch

*Library of Congress Cataloging in Publication Data*

Main entry under title: First prayers. Includes index. Summary: An illustrated collection of thirty-nine prayers, including morning and evening prayers and graces. 1. Children—Prayer-books and devotions—English.
[1. Prayers]   I. Magagna, Anna Marie, ill.   BV265.F564   1982   242′.82   82-60742   ISBN 0-02-762120-0

# FiRST pRAYERS

## Illustrated by Anna Marie Magagna

Macmillan Publishing Co., Inc. 866 Third Avenue, New York, N.Y. 10022. Collier Macmillan Canada, Inc.

Printed in the United States of America.

10 9 8 7 6 5 4 3 2 1

"Prayer for a Child" by Rachel Field is reprinted on page 52 with the permission of Macmillan Publishing Co., Inc. Copyright 1941 by Macmillan Publishing Co., Inc., renewed 1969 by Arthur S. Pederson.

"The Earth Has Got a Carpet" from *Lucie Attwell's Pop-up Book of Prayers* is reprinted on page 16 with the permission of Dean & Son Ltd. Copyright 1974 by Dean & Son Ltd.

**Macmillan Publishing Co., Inc.**
**New York**

**Collier Macmillan Publishers**
**London**

Walk, then, as children of the light.
For all you are children of the light
And children of the day.

—*Ephesians 5:8; Thessalonians 5:5*

1

This is the day which the Lord has made;
We will rejoice and be glad in it.

—*Psalm 118:24*

## In the Morning

Through the night Thine angels kept
Watch beside me while I slept.
Now the dark has gone away,
Lord, I thank Thee for this day.

—*William Canton*

## A Morning Prayer

Father in heaven, all through the night
I have been sleeping, safe in Thy sight.
Father, I thank Thee; bless me I pray,
Bless me and keep me all through the day.

—*Unknown*

4

## The Morning Bright

The morning bright,
With rosy light,
Has waked me from my sleep;
Father, I own,
Thy love alone
Thy little one doth keep.

—*Thomas O. Summers*

5

### Dawning

So here hath been dawning
Another blue day.
Think, wilt thou let it
Slip useless away?

—*Thomas Carlyle*

6

# Lamb of God, I Look to Thee

Lamb of God, I look to Thee;
Thou shalt my example be;
Thou are gentle, meek, and mild,
Thou wast once a little child.

8

Loving Jesus, gentle Lamb,
In Thy gracious hands I am,
Make me, Savior, what Thou art,
Live Thyself within my heart.
—*Charles Wesley*

9

# He Prayeth Well, Who Loveth Well

He prayeth well, who loveth well
Both man and bird and beast.

He prayeth best, who loveth best
All things both great and small;
For the dear God who loveth us,
He made and loveth all.

*—Samuel Taylor Coleridge*

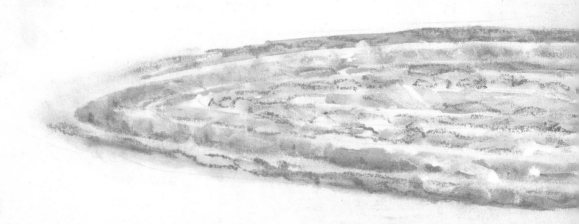

## Before I Run to Play

Now before I run to play,
    Let me not forget to pray
To God who kept me through the night
    And waked me with the morning light.

Help me, Lord, to love Thee more
    Than I ever loved before,
In my work and in my play,
    Be Thou with me through the day.

*—Unknown*

## Dear Father, Hear and Bless

Dear Father, hear and bless
Thy beasts and singing birds,
And guard with tenderness
Small things that have no words.

—*Unknown*

14

## Song

The year's at the spring
And day's at the morn;
Morning's at seven;
The hillside's dew-pearled;
The lark's on the wing;
The snail's on the thorn:
God's in His heaven—
All's right with the world!

—*Robert Browning*

# The Earth

The earth has got a carpet
All shining fresh and green.
It's made of little blades of grass
With flowers in between;

And on this carpet,
Gay and free,
We dance our thanks,
Dear Lord, to Thee.

*—Unknown*

## North, South, East, and West

North, South, East, and West,
May Thy holy name be blessed;
Everywhere beneath the sun,
May Thy holy will be done.

*—William Canton*

## Out in the Fields With God

The little cares that fretted me,
    I lost them yesterday,
Among the fields above the sea,
    Among the winds at play,
Among the lowing of the herds,
    The rustling of the trees,
Among the singing of the birds,
    The humming of the bees.

The foolish fears of what might pass,
    I cast them all away,
Among the clover-scented grass,
    Among the new-mown hay,
Among the hushing of the corn,
    Where drowsy poppies nod,
Where ill thoughts die and good are born—
    Out in the fields with God.

—*Unknown*

## Lord, Teach a Little Child to Pray

Lord, teach a little child to pray,
And then accept my prayer,
Thou hearest all the words I say
For Thou art everywhere.

A little sparrow cannot fall
Unnoticed, Lord, by Thee;
And though I am so young and small
Thou dost take care of me.

Teach me to do the thing that's right,
And when I sin, forgive;
And make it still my chief delight
To serve Thee while I live.

—*Jane Taylor*

23

## God's World

All things bright and beautiful,
  All creatures great and small,
All things wise and wonderful,
  The Lord God made them all.

24

Each little flower that opens,
    Each little bird that sings,
He made their glowing colors,
    He made their tiny wings.

The tall trees in the greenwood,
    The meadows where we play,
The rushes by the water
    We gather every day—

He gave us eyes to see them,
    And lips that we might tell
How great is God Almighty,
    Who has made all things well!

*—Mrs. Cecil F. Alexander*

### Thank You for Summer

Thank You, God, for summer
    With all its flowers gay,
And birds that sing, and green grass,
    And butterflies that play
At hide-and-seek with clover,
    And blossoms on the trees,
And sunshine bright, and showers,
    And every cooling breeze.

Yes, thank You, God, for summer;
    And always at my play
Help me, Thy child, remember
    These gifts of Thine, I pray.

                      *—Unknown*

# Grace before Meals

Be present at our table, Lord;
Be here and everywhere adored.
Thy creatures bless, and grant that we
May feast in paradise with Thee.

—*John Wesley*

# God, We Thank You

God, we thank You for this food,
For rest and home and all things good;
For wind and rain and sun above,
But most of all for those we love.

—*Maryleona Frost*

## Bless Us, O Lord

Bless us, O Lord, for these Thy gifts
Which we are about to receive
   From Thy bounty,
Through Christ our Lord.

*—Traditional*

## Thou Art Great

Thou art great and Thou art good,
And we thank Thee for this food.
By Thy hand must all be fed,
And we thank Thee for this bread.

—*Traditional*

## Father, We Thank Thee

For flowers that bloom about our feet,
    Father, we thank Thee,
For tender grass so fresh and sweet,
    Father, we thank Thee,
For the song of bird and hum of bee,
For all things fair we hear or see,
Father in heaven, we thank Thee.

For this new morning with its light,
    Father, we thank Thee,
For rest and shelter of the night,
    Father, we thank Thee,
For health and food, for love and friends,
For everything Thy goodness sends,
Father in heaven, we thank Thee.

               —*Ralph Waldo Emerson*

# Praise God

Praise God, from whom all blessings flow;
Praise Him, all creatures here below;
Praise Him above, ye heavenly host:
Praise Father, Son, and Holy Ghost.

—*Thomas Ken*

## The Gift

What can I give Him,
    Poor as I am?
If I were a shepherd,
    I would bring Him a lamb;

If I were a wise man,
    I would do my part.
But what can I give Him?
    Give Him my heart.

—*Christina Rossetti*

Glory to God in the highest,
and on earth peace, good will toward men.

—Luke 2: 14

Serve the Lord with gladness;
Come before His presence with singing.

—*Psalm 100:2*

The wolf also shall dwell
   With the lamb,
And the leopard shall lie down
   With the kid;
And a little child shall lead them.

*—Isaiah 11:6*

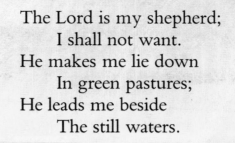

The Lord is my shepherd;
    I shall not want.
He makes me lie down
    In green pastures;
He leads me beside
    The still waters.

Surely goodness and mercy
    Shall follow me
All the days of my life:
And I shall dwell in the house
    Of the Lord forever.

*—Psalm 23:1–2,6*

# The Lord's Prayer

Our Father, who art in heaven,
Hallowed be Thy name.
Thy kingdom come;
Thy will be done
On earth as it is in heaven.
Give us this day our daily bread,
And forgive us our debts,
As we forgive our debtors.

And lead us not into temptation,
But deliver us from evil.
For Thine is the kingdom,
And the power, and the glory,
For ever.

*—New Testament*

## Dear God

Dear God,
Be good to me.
The sea is so wide
And my boat is so small.

—*Prayer of a fisherman*

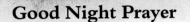

## Good Night Prayer

Father, unto Thee I pray,
Thou hast guarded me all day;
Safe I am while in Thy sight,
Safely let me sleep tonight.

Bless my friends, the whole world bless;
Help me to learn helpfulness;
Keep me ever in Thy sight;
So to all I say good night.

—*Henry Johnstone*

### Jesus, Tender Shepherd

Jesus, tender Shepherd, hear me;
Bless Thy little lamb tonight;
Through the darkness be Thou near me,
Keep me safe till morning light.

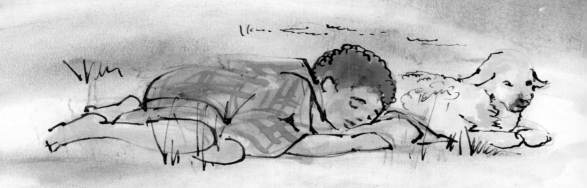

All this day Thy hand has led me,
And I thank Thee for Thy care;
Thou has warmed me, clothed and fed me;
Listen to my evening prayer.

Let my sins all be forgiven;
Bless the friends I love so well:
Take us all at last to heaven,
Happy there with Thee to dwell.

—*Mary Duncan*

## Now the Day Is Over

Now the day is over,
Night is drawing nigh,
Shadows of the evening
Steal across the sky;

Jesus, give the weary
Calm and sweet repose;
With Thy tenderest blessing
May our eyelids close.

Through the long night watches,
May Thine angels spread
Their white wings above me,
Watching round my bed.

When the morning wakens,
Then may I arise
Pure and fresh and sinless
In Thy holy eyes.

—*Sabine Baring-Gould*

51

### Prayer for a Child

Bless this milk and bless this bread.
Bless this soft and waiting bed
Where I presently shall be
Wrapped in sweet security.
Through the darkness, through the night
Let no danger come to fright
My sleep till morning once again
Beckons at the windowpane.

Bless the toys whose shapes I know,
The shoes that take me to and fro
Up and down and everywhere.
Bless my little painted chair.

Bless the lamplight, bless the fire,
Bless the hands that never tire
In their loving care of me.
Bless my friends and family.
Bless my Father and my Mother
And keep us close to one another.

Bless other children, far and near,
And keep them safe and free from fear.
So let me sleep and let me wake
In peace and health, for Jesus' sake.

—*Rachel Field*

## Good Night

Good night! Good night!
Far flies the light;
But still God's love
Shall flame above,
Making all bright.
Good night! Good night!

—*Victor Hugo*

### The Moon

I see the moon,
And the moon sees me;
God bless the moon,
And God bless me.

—*Unknown*

## Now I Lay Me Down to Sleep

Now I lay me down to sleep,
I pray Thee, Lord, Thy child to keep;
Thy love go with me all the night,
And wake me with the morning light.

—*Unknown*

## Be Near Me, Lord Jesus

Be near me, Lord Jesus, I ask Thee to stay,
Close by me forever, and love me, I pray.
Bless all the dear children in Thy tender care,
And take us to heaven, to live with Thee there.

—*Martin Luther*

# INDEX OF FIRST LINES